A PREMARITAL GUIDE FOR COUPLES

And Their Counselors

A PREMARITAL GUIDE FOR COUPLES

And Their Counselors

DAVID A. THOMPSON

BETHANY HOUSE PUBLISHERS
MINNEAPOLIS, MINNESOTA 55438
A Division of Bethany Fellowship, Inc.

A Premarital Guide for Couples and Their Counselors
Copyright © 1979
David A. Thompson

All scripture references are taken from the
King James Version of the Bible.

ISBN 0-87123-465-3

Published by Bethany House Publishers
A Ministry of Bethany Fellowship International
11400 Hampshire Avenue South
Minneapolis, Minnesota 55438
www.bethanyhouse.com

Printed in the United States of America by
Bethany Press International, Minneapolis, Minnesota 55438

Dedication

To my late parents, Arne and Hilma Thompson, who showed me that marriage can work and can bring great joy and satisfaction, and

To my dear wife, Judy, who risked saying "I do," and, as a result, has brought much color, beauty, and music into my world,

I lovingly dedicate this book.

DAVID A. THOMPSON is a chaplain serving in the United States Navy. He has been a parish pastor, hospital chaplain, Bible school teacher, and assistant editor for a religious book publisher.

He received a B.S. from the University of Wisconsin (Superior) in 1968; attended Trinity Evangelical Divinity School and the Lutheran Brethren Seminary, graduating from the latter with a M.Div. degree in 1971, and received a M.S.E. degree in Counseling from the University of Wisconsin (Oshkosh) in 1976. He is an ordained minister of the Free Methodist Church of North America. He is married and the father of three boys.

Table of Contents

SECTION I: WHERE WE BEGAN

SECTION II: WHAT WE SHARE TOGETHER

SECTION III: WHAT WE VALUE

SECTION IV: WHAT WE CAN AFFORD

SECTION V: WHAT WE SEE IN THE FUTURE

SECTION VI: WHAT WE WANT IN OUR WEDDING

How To Use This Book

FOR COUPLES: Ideally this book is designed to be used by couples either by themselves or with the assistance of a counselor or clergyman.

If used alone, without professional help, I recommend that the prospective bride and bridegroom work on each section individually (except for the budget in Section IV and the wedding details in Section VI) and then compare sheets, looking for similarities and differences. Each couple should see a pattern of compatibility/incompatibility, which should help them discuss and decide on the wisdom of saying "I do."

I would recommend, if possible, that this book be used with the assistance of a counselor or clergyman. Each section should be filled out and given to the counselor or clergyman, preferably a day or two before each session. This gives him the opportunity to become familiar with you and your needs.

FOR COUNSELORS: This premarital counseling guide is designed for six, one-hour sessions (or compressed into four sessions by combining Sections III and IV and Sections V and VI). It seeks to cut down on your time by briefly touching on areas that need little attention, and by highlighting areas that require more extensive counseling efforts. You should be looking for a compatibility/incompatibility pattern as well as background issues that may have a bearing on the prospective marriage of this couple.

Perhaps you could suggest to the couple that they pay a fee to cover the cost of materials. In that way, it concretely commits the couple, through their monetary contribution, to work at the counseling program. The other option would be to make budgetary allowances in your organization to cover the cost of materials for the estimated number of couples you will counsel in a given year.

I recommend that you set up six sessions and give the couple their book at the time of requesting an appointment for a premarital interview. They should be instructed to work on each section individually (except the budget in Section IV and all of Section VI, which should be done together). Prior to each session, have each counselee tear out the appropriate section and mail it to you in time to be received a day or two before the actual session. This will allow you time to review their responses and provide the direction for each interview. As the couple prepares to leave following each session, briefly outline their homework for the next session.

This premarital guide, set up for a number of sessions, should combat the pressure on clergy to perform a "hasty wedding." By making a policy of a six-week, six-session premarital counseling program (or optional four-session program), you will implicitly inform each couple and the community-at-large that you regard marriage as a serious business, not to be entered into lightly by anyone.

The author provides the forms in this manual for the assistance of couples, counselors, and clergy. He will not be responsible for how they are used. He trusts that they will be used to help couples discuss marriage frankly. He hopes that through this program each person contemplating marriage will make sound choices before he says, "I do."

SECTION I

Where We Began

"Therefore shall a man leave his father and his mother and shall cleave unto his wife . . ."
Genesis 2:24a

Where We Began

Much of life is like reading a good book; we are repeatedly coming to the end of one chapter and to the beginning of a new chapter. How we approach each new chapter depends on our past experiences. If past chapters of our lives have brought fulfillment, we usually look toward the future pages with hope and anticipation. On the other hand, if the foregoing chapters have brought great disappointment, we look toward forthcoming events with insecurity, even fear.

In one sense, we leave our past as we forsake father and mother and cleave to our husband or wife. Yet, in another sense, our childhood experiences and parental upbringing cling to us in the midst of cleaving to another.

This section will help you focus on those memories that cling to you. Some of those memories will help you in your new marriage, and perhaps some of your past will hinder that new relationship you are building. Allow this section to help you understand yourself best by answering each question as honestly and completely as possible.

PERSONAL HISTORY
Prospective Bridegroom

General Information

Name: _____ Birthdate: _____

Address: _____ Age: _____

Phone: Home _____ Business _____

Marital Status: Never been married   _____

Married   _____

Separated   _____

Widowed   _____

Divorced   _____

Occupation:_____ Years at that job _____

Name and address of employer   _____

_____

Education: Last year completed   _____

Degree / Diploma   _____

Major and minor (if college)   _____

Other Training: Type   _____

Number of years_____

Military Service: Branch _____ Rank _____

Number of years_____ Type of discharge _____

Special training _____

Have you ever been arrested? Yes _____ No _____

If yes, explain. _____

_____

Did someone refer you to this pastor or counselor? Yes _____ No _____

    If yes, give name and address of that person _____

_____

Health Status

Describe your general health:

    Very good _____ Good _____ Average _____ Poor _____

Describe all important present or past illnesses or handicaps:

_____

_____

_____

When was your last physical exam? _____ Results _____

_____

Who is your present physician?   Name _____

    Address _____

Are you presently taking medication?   Yes _____ No _____

    If yes, what kind and for what purpose? _____

_____

Have you ever been under treatment for emotional problems?

    Yes _____ No _____ If yes, describe when, where, and under whose care. _____

_____

Have you ever or are you presently using agents that may induce chemical dependency?

    Yes _____ No _____   If yes, what drug have you used or what are you presently using? __

_____

Personal Attributes

Describe yourself in terms of personal characteristics:

a) Positive traits: _____

_____

b) Negative traits: _____

_____

Describe the *worst* thing that ever happened to you: _____

_____

_____

_____

_____

Describe the *best* thing that *ever* happened to you:_____

_____

_____

_____

_____

Describe the person who had the greatest influence on your life: _____

_____

_____

FAMILY HISTORY   *Prospective Bridegroom*

Father   Name:_____ Living or deceased? _____

           Occupation: _____ Age: _____

           Education (highest grade completed): _____

           Marital Status: Married _____ Separated _____

                          Divorced _____ Widowed _____

           Marital History: Has your father ever been separated _____

                          divorced _____ or widowed? _____

Mother   Name:_____ Living or deceased? _____

           Occupation: _____ Age: _____

           Education (highest grade completed): _____

           Marital Status: Married _____ Separated _____

                          Divorced _____ Widowed _____

           Marital History: Has your mother ever been separated _____

                          divorced _____ or widowed? _____

Description of Your Parents

Father's character traits:

   Positive: _____

_____

   Negative: _____

_____

Mother's character traits:

   Positive: _____

_____

   Negative: _____

_____

In what ways would you want to be like your parents?

Like your father? _____

_____

Like your mother? _____

_____

In what ways would you want to be different from your parents?

Different from your father? _____

_____

Different from your mother? _____

_____

Description of Your Parents' Relationship

Describe what you observed in the following areas of your parents' relationship:

Friendship / Companionship:

General characteristics: _____

_____

Frequency of being together: _____

_____

Intensity of Relationship (competitive, combative, cool, casual, affectionate, romantic, etc.): _____

_____

Sexual Relationship: (Did you observe hugging, kissing, fondling, using endearing words, compliments, etc.?) _____

_____

Decision-making / Leadership Roles: (Who led and in what ways?) _____

_____

_____

Religious Training in the Home: (Who trained and how?) _____

_____

_____

Management of Finances: (Who managed the money, what did they do with the money, and how successful were they in this task?) _____

_____

_____

What *three* qualities in your parents' marriage would you like to duplicate in your marriage?

1) _____

2) _____

3) _____

What *three* aspects of your parents' marriage would you *not* want to duplicate in your marriage?

1) _____

2) _____

3) _____

Describe your relationships with your brothers and sisters during your childhood years: _____

_____

_____

Describe any major marital crises in your parents' marriage:

The conflict(s): _____

The reason for the conflict(s): _____

The resolution of the conflict(s): _____

Describe your feelings during this time: _____

_____

Are your feelings different now? _____

_____

Were there any chemical dependency problems (either drugs or alcohol) in your family (parents, brothers, sisters)?

Yes _____ No _____

If yes, how has that problem affected you? _____

_____

_____

DATING HISTORY   *Prospective Bridegroom*

How did you meet? _____

_____

How long have you known each other? _____

How long have you dated? _____

How long have you been engaged? _____

How soon do you plan to be married? _____

Did you date others prior to meeting your fiancee? Yes _____ No _____

If yes, how many others have you dated? _____ For how long? _____

Have you been engaged before? _____ If yes, did the prior engagement result in marriage? _____

If it did not, what ended the engagement? _____

_____

Do you love one another? _____

If yes, what do you mean when you say you "love" someone? _____

_____

Why are you getting married? (List *five* reasons in their order of importance to you.)

1) _____

2) _____

3) _____

4) _____

5) _____

What do you expect of marriage? Finish this statement:

"I expect to *get* 1) _____

2) _____

3) _____

"I expect to *give* 1) _____

2) _____

3) _____

In what ways do you think you will be a better person married than you could be by remaining single? _____
_____
_____

Describe what you believe should be the husband's role in marriage. Be as specific as possible. _____
_____
_____
_____

Describe what you believe should be the wife's role in marriage. Be as specific as possible. _____
_____
_____
_____

Counselor's Additional Questions:

PERSONAL HISTORY

Prospective Bride

General Information

Name: _____ Birthdate: _____

Address: _____ Age: _____

Phone: Home _____ Business _____

Marital Status: Never been married   _____

                   Married   _____

                   Separated   _____

                   Widowed   _____

                   Divorced   _____

Occupation: _____ Years at that job _____

    Name and address of employer   _____

                                      _____

Education: Last year completed   _____

              Degree / Diploma   _____

              Major and minor (if college)   _____

Other Training: Type _____

                  Number of Years _____

Military Service: Branch _____ Rank _____

                  Number of years _____ Type of discharge _____

                  Special training _____

Have you ever been arrested?   Yes _____ No _____

    If yes, explain. _____

                       _____

Did someone refer you to this pastor or counselor?   Yes _____ No _____

    If yes, give name and address of that person _____

    _____

Health Status

Describe your general health:

    Very good _____ Good _____ Average _____ Poor _____

Describe all important present or past illnesses or handicaps:

_____

_____

_____

When was your last physical exam? _____ Results _____

_____

Have you ever been under treatment for emotional problems? Yes _____ No _____

    If yes, describe when, where, and under whose care. _____

    _____

Have you ever or are you presently using agents that may induce chemical dependency?

    Yes _____ No _____

    If yes, what drug have you used or what are you presently using? _____

    _____

Personal Attributes

Describe yourself in terms of personal characteristics:

a) Positive traits: _____

    _____

b) Negative traits: _____

    _____

Describe the *worst* thing that ever happened to you: _____

_____

_____

_____

_____

Describe the *best* thing that ever happened to you: _____

_____

_____

_____

_____

Describe the person who had the greatest influence on your life: _____

_____

_____

_____

FAMILY HISTORY   *Prospective Bride*

Father   Name:_____ Living or deceased? _____

           Occupation: _____ Age: _____

           Education (highest grade completed): _____

Marital Status: Married _____ Separated _____

Divorced _____ Widowed _____

Marital History: Has your father ever been separated _____

divorced _____ or widowed? _____

Mother   Name:_____ Living or deceased? _____

Occupation: _____ Age: _____

Education (highest grade completed):_____

Marital Status: Married _____ Separated _____

Divorced _____ Widowed _____

Marital History: Has your mother ever been separated _____

divorced _____ or widowed? _____

Description of Your Parents

Father's character traits:

Positive: _____

_____

Negative: _____

_____

Mother's character traits:

Positive: _____

_____

Negative: _____

_____

In what ways would you want to be like your parents?

Like your father? _____

_____

Like your mother? _____

_____

In what ways would you want to be different from your parents?

Different from your father?_____

_____

Different from your mother? _____

_____

Description of Your Parents' Relationship

Describe what you observed in the following areas of your parents' relationship:

Friendship / Companionship:

   General characteristics: _____

_____

   Frequency of being together: _____

_____

   Intensity of Relationship (competitive, combative, cool, casual, affectionate, romantic, etc.): _____

_____

Sexual Relationship: (Did you observe hugging, kissing, fondling, using endearing words, compliments, etc.?) _____

_____

Decision-making / Leadership Roles: (Who led and in what ways?) _____

_____

_____

Religious Training in the Home: (Who trained and how?) _____

_____

_____

Management of Finances: (Who managed the money, what did they do with the money, and how successful were they in this task? _____

_____

What *three* qualities in your parents' marriage would you like to duplicate in your marriage?

   1) _____

   2) _____

   3) _____

What *three* aspects of your parents' marriage would you *not* want to duplicate in your marriage?

   1) _____

   2) _____

   3) _____

Describe your relationships with your brothers and sisters during your childhood years: _____

_____

_____

Describe any major marital crises in your parents' marriage:

   The conflict(s): _____

   The reason for the conflict(s): _____

   The resolution of the conflict(s): _____

   Describe your feelings during this time: _____

_____

   Are your feelings different now? Explain. _____

_____

Were there any chemical dependency problems (either drugs or alcohol) in your family (parents, brothers, sisters)?

Yes _____ No _____

If yes, how has that problem affected you?_____

_____

_____

DATING HISTORY

Prospective Bride

How did you meet? _____

_____

How long have you known each other? _____

How long have you dated? _____

How long have you been engaged? _____

How soon do you plan to be married? _____

Did you date others prior to meeting your fiance? Yes _____ No _____

If yes, how many others have you dated? _____ For how long? _____

Have you been engaged before? _____ If yes, did the prior engagement result in marriage? _____

If it did not, what ended the engagement?_____

_____

Do you love one another? _____

If yes, what do you mean when you say you "love" someone? _____

_____

Why are you getting married? (List *five* reasons in their order of importance to you.)

1) _____

2) _____

3) _____

4) _____

5) _____

What do you expect of marriage? Finish this statement:

"I expect to *get*   1) _____

2) _____

3) _____

"I expect to *give*   1) _____

2) _____

3) _____

In what ways do you think you will be a better person married than you could be by remaining single? _____
_____
_____

Describe what you believe should be the husband's role in marriage. Be as specific as possible. _____
_____
_____
_____

Describe what you believe should be the wife's role in marriage. Be as specific as possible. _____
_____
_____
_____

Counselor's Additional Questions:

SECTION II

What We Share Together

" . . . and they shall be one flesh."
Genesis 2:24b

What We Share Together

To become one flesh is to be known more intimately than you have ever been known before. It involves, as it did for that first couple in the Garden of Eden, the ability to stand before one another naked and not be ashamed. Certainly this passage speaks of more than mere sexual intimacy; it refers also to the sharing of all other aspects of our lives, without seeking a cover, without shame or embarrassment.

"Becoming one" is not easy. We bring to the marriage relationship two unique ways of thinking and responding. These need to be harmonized in order to make our marriage successful. We constantly recognize that we are flesh; our spouse is very human and fallible. So, be patient with one another as you learn this process of sharing your life together.

This section will highlight some areas where the two of you will be learning to become one flesh. Answer each question as clearly and thoroughly as you can.

COMMUNICATION   *Prospective Bridegroom*

What subjects have you talked about? Be as specific as possible, listing the subjects in the order of their importance (education, career goals, financial planning, family planning, etc.).

1) _____
2) _____
3) _____
4) _____
5) _____
6) _____
7) _____
8) _____

Who does the most talking when you are alone? _____

What do you do to let your fiancee know that you are angry?_____
_____
_____

What kind of disagreements have you had? _____
_____
_____

What have you done to resolve your differences? _____
_____
_____

When you become bothered about something, how do you react? (Blow up or withdraw? Yell or cry? Seek quick resolution or engage in prolonged pouting?) _____
_____
_____

In what ways has your fiancee communicated to you changes that she would like to make in your life?

    a) List the changes: _____

_____

_____

    b) How has she communicated this? _____

_____

_____

What are your feelings toward these changes? _____

_____

_____

Have you expressed your feelings concerning these proposed changes? _____

    In what ways? _____

_____

    With what results? _____

_____

What changes have you shared with your fiancee that you would like her to make? _____

_____

_____

What were her reactions to these proposed changes? _____

_____

_____

SEX

Prospective Bridegroom

*Counselor: Discuss the limits of confidentiality regarding this section with the couple.

Do you know of any reason why you cannot have a normal sex life (damage to sexual organs by accident, disease, or organic malfunction)? _____

_____

Do you know of any reason why conception would not be possible due to impotence or other physiological problem? _____

_____

Have you ever had any form of venereal disease? _____

    If yes, explain. _____

_____

State any fears you have concerning sexual intimacy: _____

_____

_____

_____

Have you ever been molested, raped, subject to indecent exposure or homosexual encounter/relations? _____ If yes, explain what happened (when it happened and what effect you feel this will have on your future marital relations): _____

_____

_____

What impressed you positively or negatively about your parents' sexual relationship? _____

_____

_____

Do you feel adequately informed about sexual processes? Yes _____ No _____ What is the extent of your sex education and from what sources did your information come? _____

_____

_____

Have you talked about sex with your fiancee? Yes _____ No _____ Explain. _____

_____

_____

_____

State areas where you feel you still have questions concerning sex: _____

_____

_____

_____

What do you think is the purpose of sex in marriage? _____

_____

What do you expect to give and receive in your sexual relationship? _____

_____

Do you look forward to sex in your marriage? Yes ____ No ____ Why? _____

_____

Describe any discussions you have had with your parents about sex. _____

_____

Do you feel that previous sexual encounters can have an effect on a marriage? If so, in what way? _____

_____

Do you believe in birth control? Yes _____ No _____

    If yes, who do you feel is responsible for contraception? _____

    Also, if you believe in contraception, what method(s) have you discussed and chosen for yourselves? _____

_____

_____

Would you consider abortion? Yes _____ No _____

    If yes, under what circumstances? _____

_____

CHILDREN

Are you planning to have children? Yes _____ No _____

    If no, explain. _____

_____

Do you know of any physiological or psychological reason why you cannot or should not have children?

    Yes _____ No _____ If yes, explain. _____

_____

How many children would you like to have? _____

When would you like to have them? _____

What do you believe is an ideal spacing between children? _____

_____

In what ways do you believe the husband should be involved in the raising of children? (Be specific.) _____

_____

_____

_____

_____

_____

In what ways do you believe the wife should be involved in the raising of children? (Be specific.) _____

_____

_____

_____

_____

_____

Do you believe in the concept of the "working mother"

    a) during the children's pre-school years? _____

    b) during the childhood years? _____

Who should bear the responsibility for disciplining the children? _____

What methods of discipline are you planning to use with your children? _____

_____

_____

_____

_____

_____

I want to teach my children the following values: (List in order of their importance.)

1) _____

2) _____

3) _____

4) _____

5) _____

What will you do to instill these values? (Be specific.) _____

_____

_____

_____

If you cannot have children, what are your feelings regarding adoption? _____

_____

_____

IN-LAWS   *Prospective Bridegroom*

Briefly describe your future in-laws (mother-in-law and father-in-law), listing important positive and negative traits:

Things I especially like about them: _____

_____

_____

Things I don't particularly like about them: _____

_____

_____

What do you believe your future in-laws' feelings are toward you and your impending marriage into the family? ___

_____

What do you see as potential points of conflict with your in-laws (cultural differences, religious differences, etc.)? ___

_____

_____

What do you think you can do to resolve these areas of conflict? _____

_____

_____

_____

What will be the frequency and the extent of your future in-laws' involvement in your new life as a couple? _____

_____

_____

Counselor's Additional Questions:

COMMUNICATION

What subjects have you talked about? Be as specific as possible, listing the subjects in the order of their importance to you (education, career goals, financial planning, family planning, etc.).

1) _____
2) _____
3) _____
4) _____
5) _____
6) _____
7) _____
8) _____

Who does the most talking when you are alone? _____

What do you do to let your fiance know that you are angry? _____
_____
_____

What kind of disagreements have you had? _____
_____
_____

What have you done to resolve your differences? _____
_____
_____

When you become bothered about something, how do you react? (Blow up or withdraw? Yell or cry? Seek quick resolution or engage in prolonged pouting?) _____
_____
_____

In what ways has your fiance communicated to you changes that he would like to make in your life?

a) List the changes: _____
_____
_____

b) How has he communicated this? _____
_____
_____

What are your feelings toward these changes? _____
_____
_____

32

Have you expressed your feelings concerning these proposed changes? _____

    In what ways? _____

_____

    With what results? _____

_____

What changes have you shared with your fiance that you would like him to make? _____

_____

_____

What were his reactions to these proposed changes? _____

_____

_____

SEX *Prospective Bride*

*Counselor: Discuss the limits of confidentiality regarding this section with the couple.

Do you know any reason why you cannot have a normal sex life (damage to sexual organs by accident, disease, or organic malfunction)? _____

_____

Do you know any reason why conception would not be possible due to impotence or other physiological problem? _____

Have you ever had any form of venereal disease? _____

    If yes, explain. _____

    _____

State any fears you have concerning sexual intimacy: _____

_____

_____

Have you ever been molested, raped, subject to indecent exposure, or homosexual encounter/relations? _____

    If yes, explain what happened (when it happened and what effect you feel this will have on your future marital relations): _____

    _____

    _____

What impressed you positively or negatively about your parents' sexual relationship? _____

_____

_____

Do you feel adequately informed about sexual processes? Yes _____ No _____

What is the extent of your sex education and from what sources did your information come (books, friends, parents, etc.)? _____

_____

_____

Have you talked about sex with your fiance? Yes_____ No _____

Explain. _____

_____

_____

State areas where you feel you still have questions concerning sex: _____

_____

_____

What do you think is the purpose of sex in marriage? _____

_____

What do you expect to give and receive in your sexual relationship? _____

_____

Do you look forward to sex in your marriage? Yes ____ No ____ Why? _____

_____

Describe any discussions you have had with your parents about sex. _____

_____

Do you feel that previous sexual encounters can have an effect on a marriage? If so, in what way? _____

_____

Do you believe in birth control? Yes _____ No _____

If yes, who do you feel is responsible for contraception? _____

Also, if you believe in contraception, what method(s) have you discussed and chosen for yourselves? _____

_____

_____

Would you consider abortion? Yes _____ No _____

If yes, under what circumstances? _____

_____

_____

CHILDREN

Prospective Bride

Are you planning to have children? Yes _____ No _____

If no, explain. _____

_____

Do you know of any physiological or psychological reason why you cannot or should not have children?

Yes _____ No _____ If yes, explain. _____

_____

_____

How many children would you like to have? _____

When would you like to have them? _____

What do you believe is an ideal spacing between children? _____

_____

In what ways do you believe the husband should be involved in the raising of children? (Be specific.) _____

_____

_____

_____

_____

_____

In what ways do you believe the wife should be involved in the raising of children? (Be specific.) _____

_____

_____

_____

_____

_____

Do you believe in the concept of the "working mother"

    a) during the children's pre-school years? _____

    b) during the childhood years? _____

Who should bear the responsibility for disciplining the children? _____

What methods of discipline are you planning to use with your children? _____

_____

I want to teach my children the following values: (List in order of their importance.)

    1) _____

    2) _____

    3) _____

    4) _____

    5) _____

What will you do to instill these values? (Be specific.) _____

_____

_____

_____

If you cannot have children, what are your feelings regarding adoption? _____

_____

_____

IN-LAWS   *Prospective Bride*

Briefly describe your future in-laws (mother-in-law and father-in-law), listing important positive and negative traits:

Things I especially like about them: _____

_____

_____

Things I don't particularly like about them: _____

_____

_____

What do you believe your future in-laws' feelings are toward you and your impending marriage into the family? ___

_____

What do you see as potential points of conflict with your in-laws (cultural differences, religious differences, etc.)? ___

_____

_____

What do you think you can do to resolve these areas of conflict? _____

_____

_____

_____

What will be the frequency and the extent of your future in-laws' involvement in your new life as a couple? _____

_____

_____

Counselor's Additional Questions:

SECTION III

What We Value

"But seek ye first the kingdom of God, and his righteousness; and all these things shall be added unto you."
Matthew 6:33

What We Value

What is really important in life? There are so many things vying for our attention, time, and money. As a couple, you will have to make choices that will shape the direction of your lives. Recognize that it is the little, day-by-day decisions that lead you into a path of fulfillment or into a way of disappointment.

Use this section to measure your values so that you will make wise choices, ones with lasting value. Attempt to crystalize your thinking regarding what is most important to you. Based on that assessment, you must establish priorities among the many options available to you. Be aware that it is difficult—perhaps even impossible—for mere *things* to satisfy our deepest needs. Only people, whom God made in His own image, have an eternal value.

GOALS AND VALUES   *Prospective Bridegroom*

In one brief paragraph, tell what are your purposes for living:

_____

_____

_____

_____

_____

List in order of importance and time priority *five* goals that you are seeking to reach in your lifetime:

1) _____

2) _____

3) _____

4) _____

5) _____

How do you hope to achieve these goals? (List specific plans.)

1) _____

2) _____

3) _____

4) _____

5) _____

6) _____

7) _____

8) _____

9) _____

10) _____

In what ways are your goals

a) the same as your fiancee's goals? _____

b) In what ways are they different? _____
_____
_____

In what ways do you hope to resolve goal differences with your fiancee? _____
_____
_____

What were the goals of your parents and how well have they done in achieving them? _____
_____
_____
_____

What are "must items" in terms of how much money you make and what kind of a life-style you lead (kind of house, car , clothes, friends, entertainment, etc.)? _____
_____
_____
_____
_____

If you had to make a choice between working long hours to make a lot of money (and thus have less time together as a couple) and working shorter hours and having less money (though more time together), which would you choose? _____
Explain your answer. _____
_____
_____

RELIGION   *Prospective Bridegroom*

Briefly describe your parents' religious background in terms of religious affiliation and depth of religious commitment:
Father: _____
_____
Mother: _____
_____

How often do you go to church? _____
How often do you read your Bible? _____
How often do you pray? _____
Do you have a devotional time with your fiancee? Yes _____ No _____ If yes, how often? _____
What do you believe it means to be a Christian? _____
_____
_____

Would you characterize yourself as a Christian? Yes _____ No _____

    If yes, what basis do you have for making such a statement? _____

_____

_____

Would you say that your fiancee is a Christian? Yes _____ No _____

On what basis have you made that judgment? _____

_____

Have you been baptized? Yes _____ No _____

    If yes, when? _____

Describe a time when you felt very close to God: _____

_____

_____

_____

Describe a time when you felt very far from God: _____

_____

_____

_____

Describe where you believe you are now in your relationship to God: _____

_____

_____

_____

What issue(s) is God dealing with right now in your life that keeps you on the "growing edge" spiritually? _____

_____

_____

Describe the level of religious commitment you believe your fiancee to have: _____

_____

Do you see any areas of conflict on spiritual issues with your fiancee? Yes _____ No _____

    Explain. _____

_____

_____

What do you think constitutes a truly Christian marriage? _____

_____

_____

Who do you believe is responsible for spiritual leadership in the home? _____

    How does that affect you? _____

_____

_____

Write a brief autobiography of your spiritual life to date: _____

_____

_____

_____

_____

_____

Counselor's Additional Questions:

GOALS AND VALUES

In one brief paragraph, tell what are your purposes for living: _____

_____

_____

_____

_____

_____

_____

List in order of importance and time priority *five* goals that you are seeking to reach in your lifetime:

1) _____
2) _____
3) _____
4) _____
5) _____

How do you hope to achieve these goals? (List specific plans.)

1) _____
2) _____
3) _____
4) _____
5) _____
6) _____
7) _____
8) _____
9) _____
10) _____

In what ways are your goals

a) the same as your fiance's goals? _____

_____

_____

b) In what ways are they different? _____

_____

_____

In what ways do you hope to resolve goal differences with your fiance? _____

_____

_____

44

What were the goals of your parents and how well have they done in achieving them? _____

_____

_____

_____

What are "must items" in terms of how much money you make and what kind of a life-style you lead (kind of house, car, clothes, friends, entertainment, etc.)? _____

_____

_____

_____

_____

_____

If you had to make a choice between working long hours to make a lot of money (and thus have less time together as a couple) and working shorter hours and having less money (though more time together), which would you choose? _____

Explain your answer: _____

_____

_____

RELIGION

Prospective Bride

Briefly describe your parents' religious background in terms of religious affiliation and depth of religious commitment:

Father: _____

_____

Mother: _____

_____

How often do you go to church? _____

How often do you read your Bible? _____

How often do you pray? _____

Do you have a devotional time with your fiance? Yes _____ No _____

If yes, how often? _____

What do you believe it means to be a Christian? _____

_____

_____

Would you characterize yourself as a Christian? Yes _____ No _____

If yes, what basis do you have for making such a statement? _____

_____

_____

Would you say that your fiance is a Christian? Yes _____ No _____

On what basis have you made that judgment? _____

_____

Have you been baptized? Yes _____ No _____

If yes, when? _____

Describe a time when you felt very close to God: _____

_____

_____

_____

Describe a time when you felt very far from God: _____

_____

_____

_____

Describe where you believe you are now in your relationship to God: _____

_____

_____

_____

What issue(s) is God dealing with right now in your life that keeps you on the "growing edge" spiritually? _____

_____

_____

Describe the level of religious commitment you believe your fiance to have: _____

_____

Do you see any areas of conflict on spiritual issues with your fiance? Yes _____ No _____

Explain. _____

_____

What do you think constitutes a truly Christian marriage? _____

_____

_____

Who do you believe is responsible for spiritual leadership in the home? _____ How does that affect you?

_____

_____

_____

Write a brief autobiography of your spiritual life to date: _____
_____
_____
_____
_____
_____

Counselor's Additional Questions:

SECTION IV

What We Can Afford

"Lay not up for yourselves treasures upon earth where moth and rust doth corrupt, and where thieves break through and steal. But lay up for yourselves treasures in heaven. . . . For where your treasure is, there will your heart be also."
Matthew 6:19-21

What We Can Afford

Making the right investments is very important to most of us. Jesus, in His Sermon on the Mount, addresses the need to invest in those things that last. So many things on which we spend our money rust and decay. They can be stolen from us by unprincipled thieves or they can disappear during a time of unfavorable economic conditions. Only those investments made in people, with an eye to eternal dividends, are wise.

Jesus clearly advises us that where we make our investment, there is the focus of our thoughts and energies. Therefore, as you plan your financial future, remember you are doing more than spending money; in a very real sense, you are making a commitment to live for the present or to invest for eternity.

Keep in mind the priorities and values you have already discussed. Then attempt to make out your budget as sensibly and realistically as possible.

FINANCIAL GOALS AND PRIORITIES   *Prospective Bridegroom*

List in order of importance *five* areas where you should spend your money right now:

1) _____   4) _____

2) _____   5) _____

3) _____

If someone gave you a gift of $5000, how would you spend it? _____

_____

_____

_____

_____

What amount of money do you think you must earn to live the kind of life-style you would like to live? _____

What would this money buy? _____

_____

_____

What are your feelings about giving to church and charity? _____

_____

_____

What percentage of your gross income do you feel is appropriate to give? _____

_____

What is your attitude toward going into debt?

a) Short-term debt (credit cards, charge accounts, etc.) _____

_____ How much? _____

b) Long-term debt (auto loans, housing loans, etc.) _____

_____

How much money will you be willing to pay for housing when you are first married?_____

_____

How much will you be willing to pay for an automobile(s) when you are first married (both purchase and mainte-nance)?_____

Do you plan to save a portion of each check? Yes _____ No _____

    If yes, what percentage do you feel is appropriate?_____

Who is going to be responsible for financial planning and bill paying in your future home?_____

What kind of insurance protection do you think you will need? (List amount of life insurance.)

Type of insurance	For you	For your fiancee
Health insurance	_____	_____
Life insurance	_____	_____
Auto insurance (for both)	Yes _____	No _____

Have you made a will? Yes _____ No _____

    If no, do you plan to do so? Yes _____ No _____ Explain. _____

    _____

    _____

What are your feelings about having a percentage of your take-home pay (after taxes and major payments) set aside as a "non-accountable allowance" for each of you to spend as you like, no questions asked? _____

_____

_____

What amount would be appropriate for each? Husband _____ Wife _____

What do you believe is the function of a budget? _____

_____

What are your feelings about budgeting? _____

_____

Counselor's Additional Questions:

FINANCIAL GOALS AND PRIORITIES   *Prospective Bride*

List in order of importance *five* areas where you should spend your money right now:

1) _____   4) _____

2) _____   5) _____

3) _____

If someone gave you a gift of $5000, how would you spend it?_____
_____
_____

What amount of money do you think you must earn to live the kind of life style you would like to live?_____

    What would this money buy?_____
_____
_____

What are your feelings about giving to church and charity?_____
_____
_____

What percentage of your gross income do you feel is appropriate to give?_____
_____

What is your attitude toward going into debt?

    1) Short-term debt (credit cards, charge accounts, etc.)_____
_____ How much? _____

    b) Long-term debt (auto loans, housing loans, etc.) _____
_____

How much money will you be willing to pay for housing when you are first married?_____
_____

How much money will you be willing to pay for an automobile(s) when you are first married (both purchase and maintenance)?_____

Do you plan to save a portion of each check? Yes _____ No _____

    If yes, what percentage do you feel is appropriate?_____

Who is going to be responsible for financial planning and bill paying in your future home?_____

What kind of insurance protection do you think you will need? (List amount of life insurance.)

Type of insurance	*For you*	*For your fiance*
Health insurance	_____	_____
Life insurance	_____	_____
Auto insurance (for both)	Yes _____	No _____

Have you made a will? Yes _____ No _____

If no, do you plan to do so? Yes _____ No _____ Explain. _____
_____

What are your feelings about having a percentage of your take-home pay (after taxes and major payments) set aside as a "non-accountable allowance" for each of you to spend as you like, no questions asked? _____
_____
_____

What amount would be appropriate for each? Husband _____ Wife _____

What do you believe is the function of a budget? _____
_____

What are your feelings about budgeting? _____
_____

Counselor's Additional Questions:

BUDGET   *Prospective Bridegroom and Bride*

Gross Income $ _____

Fixed Expenses
    Income and payroll taxes $ _____
    Social Security   _____
    Union Dues   _____
    Tithe (10% of Gross)   _____
    Other _____   _____

    _____

Total Fixed Expenses $ _____

Working Income (Deduct Total Fixed from Gross Income)

                                                $ _____

Budget %
    $ _____ Savings
        (10% of Working Income) $ _____

    $ _____ Living Expenses $ _____

	Monthly	Per Pay Period
(70% of Working Income)		
Mortgage or Rent	$ _____	$ _____
Heat	_____	_____
Electricity	_____	_____
Water/Sewage/Garbage	_____	_____
Telephone	_____	_____
Car Insurance	_____	_____
Gasoline	_____	_____
Car Repairs	_____	_____
Recreation/Entertainment	_____	_____
Newspapers/Periodicals	_____	_____
Health Insurance	_____	_____
Car Insurance	_____	_____
Life Insurance	_____	_____
Doctor, Dentist, Medications	_____	_____
Food/Household	_____	_____
Cleaning/Dry Cleaning	_____	_____
Clothes	_____	_____
Home Furnishings	_____	_____
Emergency	_____	_____
Christmas and Gifts	_____	_____
Vacation	_____	_____
Allowances	_____	_____
Other _____	_____	_____
_____	_____	_____
_____	_____	_____

TOTAL LIVING EXPENSE $ _____ $ _____

$ _____ Debts and Buffer (20% of Working Income)

_____   _____
_____   _____
_____   _____
_____   _____
_____   _____
_____   _____
_____   _____

TOTAL DEBTS $ _____ $ _____

SECTION V

What We See in the Future

"Commit thy way unto the Lord; trust also in him; and he shall bring it to pass."
Psalm 37:5

What We See in the Future

What will the future hold? As a couple looking into the future, you perhaps feel the contrasting emotions of optimism and pessimism. You are optimistic as you comprehend the love you have for each other; but sometimes you may be a little pessimistic as you look at the dismal statistics of those who stood at that altar where you are about to stand— and who failed!

If there is a key to a successful future, it is this: Give over your lives to God for His direction and correction. As you step out in this trusting act of commitment, you can be assured that the Lord will direct your paths.

God's promises are a guarantee for a satisfying future. As you plan for marriage, begin to get in the practice of testing out some of these promises. Then look with great expectation for God to answer and lead.

EMPLOYMENT/CAREER PLANS   *Prospective Bridegroom*

What gifts and/or abilities do you believe you have received?_____

_____

_____

_____

_____

What have you attempted to accomplish to date?

   a) Successful attempts: _____

       _____

       _____

   b) Unsuccessful attempts: _____

       _____

       _____

Do you like working primarily with people or with things? _____

   Explain: _____

       _____

       _____

In which subjects did you excel in school? _____

_____

In what subjects were you less than successful? _____

_____

Would you describe yourself as having strong academic skills or strong vocational skills? _____

   List some skills you possess: _____

       _____

What was your overall grade average in school (A=4.0; B=3.0; etc.)?

In high school _____ In college _____ In graduate school _____

In vocational/technical school _____ Service schools _____

Other schools _____

What was your class rank approximately? _____

What kind of jobs have you held? _____

_____

_____

What direction do these jobs seem to be leading you in terms of

a) advancement? _____

_____

b) further training? _____

_____

c) wages and benefits? _____

_____

What are your plans toward further education or technical training? _____

_____

If you desire further training, how do you propose to get this education? _____

_____

What results do you expect from this effort of achieving more training? _____

_____

How does your fiancee feel about the sacrifices you may have to make in time and money to get this education?

_____

_____

What would you want to *be* more than anything else in the world? _____

Explain. _____

_____

What are your short-term employment goals (job)? _____

_____

What is your long-term employment goal (career)? _____

_____

What effect will your employment choices have on your marriage in the next five years in terms of the following:

a) Time: _____

_____

b) Money: _____

_____

c) Relationships: _____

_____

d) Moving: _____

_____

What are your feelings about both husband and wife working? _____

_____

_____

What do you realistically hope to achieve in the next twenty years in terms of career goals? _____

_____

_____

_____

_____

_____

What issues should you be aware of in your job which could affect your marital happiness? _____

_____

_____

What steps will you take to offset "vocational stress" on your marriage? _____

_____

_____

_____

_____

_____

What do you hope to achieve by the time you retire? (Be specific.) _____

_____

_____

_____

RESIDENCE   *Prospective Bridegroom*

What kind of house or apartment would you like to have in the future? Describe your "dream house." (List special rooms, conveniences, and luxury items.) _____

_____

_____

_____

_____

Where would you like to live? _____

Why would you like to live there? _____

_____

Do you see your future residence as primarily a family retreat or as primarily a center for entertaining and socializing? _____

_____ Explain. _____

_____

_____

What home maintenance chores do you plan to do and what do you believe your future wife should do? _____

_____

_____

_____

FRIENDS/RECREATION *Prospective Bridegroom*

Who are your primary friends (school "buddies," work associates, neighbors, etc.) ? _____

_____

Who are your fiancee's and your mutual friends? _____

_____

Are most of these friends single people or married people? _____

_____

Do you expect these friendships to change after your marriage? Yes _____ No _____

Explain. _____

_____

What interests do you share with your future wife? _____

_____

Which of your interests and hobbies are not shared by your fiancee? _____

_____

What do you think you can do as a couple to make new friends? _____

_____

What qualities and interests are you looking for in people that you would like for your new friends? _____

_____

_____

List *five* things you like to do for recreation:

1) _____   4) _____

2) _____   5) _____

3) _____

What organizations do you currently belong to? _____
_____

What organizations does your fiancee currently belong to? _____
_____

Are there any organizations you plan to join as a couple (civic groups, churches, etc.)? _____
_____

What do you plan to do to keep your marriage "alive" in the years after the wedding? _____
_____
_____
_____

Counselor's Additional Questions:

EMPLOYMENT/CAREER PLANS

What gifts and/or abilities do you believe you have received? _____

_____

_____

_____

What have you attempted to accomplish to date?

    a) Successful attempts: _____

        _____

        _____

    b) Unsuccessful attempts: _____

        _____

Do you like working primarily with people or with things? _____

    Explain. _____

        _____

        _____

In which subjects did you excel, in school? _____

_____

    In which subjects were you less than successful? _____

    _____

Would you describe yourself as having strong academic skills or strong vocational skills? _____

    List some skills you possess: _____

    _____

What was your overall grade average in school (A=4.0; B=3.0, etc.)?

    In high school _____ In college _____ In graduate school _____

    In vocational/technical school _____ Service schools _____

    Other schools _____

What was your class rank approximately? _____

What kind of jobs have you held? _____

_____

What direction do these jobs seem to be leading you in terms of

    a) advancement? _____

        _____

    b) further training? _____

        _____

c) wages and benefits? _____

_____

What are your plans toward further education or technical training? _____

_____

If you desire further training, how do you propose to get this education? _____

_____

What results do you expect from this effort of achieving more training? _____

_____

How does your fiance feel about the sacrifices you may have to make in time and money to get this education? ____

_____

_____

What would you want to *be* more than anything else in the world? _____

_____ Explain. _____

_____

What are your short-term employment goals (job)? _____

_____

What is your long-term employment goal (career)? _____

_____

What effect will your employment choices have on your marriage in the next five years in terms of the following:

a) Time _____

_____

b) Money: _____

_____

c) Relationships: _____

_____

d) Moving: _____

_____

What are your feelings about both husband and wife working? _____

_____

_____

What do you realistically hope to achieve in the next twenty years in terms of career goals? _____

_____

_____

_____

_____

What issues should you be aware of in your job which could affect your marital happiness? _____

_____

_____

What steps will you take to offset "vocational stress" on your marriage? _____

_____

_____

_____

_____

What do you hope to achieve by the time you retire? (Be specific.) _____

_____

_____

_____

RESIDENCE

Prospective Bride

What kind of house or apartment would you like to have in the future? Describe your "dream house." (List special rooms, conveniences, and luxury items.) _____

_____

_____

_____

_____

Where would you like to live? _____

   Why would you like to live there? _____

   _____

   _____

Do you see your future residence as primarily a family retreat or as primarily a center for entertaining and socializing? _____

_____ Explain. _____

_____

_____

What home maintenance chores do you plan to do and what do you believe your future husband should do? _____

_____

_____

_____

FRIENDS/RECREATION

Who are your primary friends (school friends, work associates, neighbors, etc.)? _____

Who are your fiance's and your mutual friends? _____

_____

Are most of these friends single people or married people? _____

_____

Do you expect these friendships to change after your marriage? Yes _____ No _____

Explain. _____

_____

_____

_____

Which of your interests and hobbies are not shared by your fiance? _____

_____

_____

What do you think you can do as a couple to make new friends? _____

_____

_____

What qualities and interests are you looking for in people that you would like for your new friends? _____

_____

_____

List *five* things you like to do for recreation:

1) _____   4) _____

2) _____   5) _____

3) _____

What organizations do you currently belong to? _____

_____

What organizations does your fiance currently belong to? _____

_____

Are there any organizations you plan to join as a couple (civic groups, churches, etc.)? _____

_____

What do you plan to do to keep your marriage "alive" in the years after the wedding? _____

_____

_____

_____

Counselor's Additional Questions:

SECTION VI

What We Want in Our Wedding

"For where two or three are gathered together in my name, there am I in the midst of them."
Matthew 18:20

What We Want in Our Wedding

Planning for weddings can be fun, yet at times frustrating. It is a time when we feel that we are on an emotional roller coaster in the midst of a multitude of unfinished tasks. Therefore, it is vital to make provision for the Lord to enter into the center of our plans.

We can send all our engraved invitations, secure the best caterers, get the most talented musicians, and reserve the nicest stained-glass chapel—and then forget the most important thing: The Lord himself belongs in the center of the wedding service, and even more importantly, in the center of our lives.

You are planning a worship service where you are inviting God and man to participate with you as you make some very solemn vows to each other. Claim God's presence and His promises for your lives as you vow to live for Him and for each other.

VITAL INFORMATION   *Prospective Bridegroom and Bride*

Bridegroom's name as it is to appear on the marriage license: _____

Bridegroom's address: _____

Bridegroom's telephone number: _____

Bride's name as it is to appear on the marriage license: _____

Bride's address: _____

Bride's telephone number: _____

Witnesses' names and addresses: (Best Man) _____

    (age 18 or over)   (address) _____

                          (Maid of Honor) _____

                          (address) _____

Date of wedding: _____ Time:_____

Place of wedding: _____ (Church name, home, etc.)

_____ (address)

Has the church, hall, home, or outdoor location been reserved for the wedding?

Yes _____ No _____

Who is officiating: Name: _____ Phone: _____

    Address: _____

Will more than one clergyman be participating? Yes _____ No _____

If yes, list name, address, and telephone number:

    Name: _____ Phone: _____

    Address: _____

Have arrangements been made with a florist for the flowers, including altar baskets, centerpiece,

·corsages for special family members and helpers, and an aisle cloth? _____

_____

If not, what still needs to be done? _____

_____

Have all attendants been notified and made aware of any financial obligations for formal wear? _____

Have all musicians and soloists been notified? _____

Have you made provision for honorariums for official participants? _____

Have you made arrangements for a photographer? _____

WEDDING WISHES   *Prospective Bridegroom and Bride*

Do you have any special wishes concerning the wedding ceremony itself? Please explain. _____

_____

_____

_____

Do you have a special theme around which you want the ceremony planned (co-ordinate prelude, musical selections, scripture reading)? _____

_____

_____

Do you have any special passages of scripture that are especially meaningful to either of you? _____

_____

_____

Are there any special announcements that you would like the pastor to make pertaining to the reception following the ceremony? _____

_____

_____

Is there anything about your upcoming marriage, the arrangements for the wedding, or the details of the ceremony about which you are still uncertain? _____

_____

_____

_____

WEDDING BUDGET   *Prospective Bridegroom and Bride*

Amount available to spend _____

(Please do *in pencil* to allow for changes.)

Rental of Church   _____

Rental of Reception Hall   _____

Clergy Honorarium   _____

Organist Honorarium   _____

Vocalist(s) Honorarium   _____

Musicians Honorarium   _____

Rental of Male Attendants' Clothing   _____

Florist Charges   _____

Photographers' Charges   _____

Catering Charges   _____

Printing Charges (for invitations, announcements,   _____
    thank you notes, napkins, etc.)

Janitorial Fee   _____

Wedding Rings   _____

Marriage License   _____

Gifts for Attendants   _____

Medical Examinations and/or Blood Tests   _____

Honeymoon (transportation, accommodations,   _____
    food, sight-seeing, etc.)

Other _____   _____

Other _____   _____

Other _____   _____

Total Cost   _____

INVITATION LIST

(Bridegroom's Relatives and Friends)

Name	*Address*
1.	
2.	
3.	
4.	
5.	
6.	
7.	
8.	
9.	
10.	
11.	
12.	
13.	
14.	
15.	
16.	
17.	
18.	
19.	
20.	
21.	
22.	
23.	
24.	
25.	
26.	
27.	
28.	
29.	
30.	
31.	
32.	
33.	

INVITATION LIST (Cont.)

(Bridegroom's Relatives and Friends)

Name   *Address*

34.

35.

36.

37.

38.

39.

40.

41.

42.

43.

44.

45.

46.

47.

48.

49.

50.

51.

52.

53.

54.

55.

56.

57.

58.

59.

60.

61.

62.

63.

64.

65.

66.

INVITATION LIST (Cont.)

(Bridegroom's Relatives and Friends)

Name   *Address*

67.

68.

69.

70.

71.

72.

73.

74.

75.

76.

77.

78.

79.

80.

81.

82.

83.

84.

85.

86.

87.

88.

89.

90.

91.

92.

93.

94.

95.

96.

97.

98.

99.

100.

INVITATION LIST

(Bride's Relatives and Friends)

	Name	*Address*
1.		
2.		
3.		
4.		
5.		
6.		
7.		
8.		
9.		
10.		
11.		
12.		
13.		
14.		
15.		
16.		
17.		
18.		
19.		
20.		
21.		
22.		
23.		
24.		
25.		
26.		
27.		
28.		
29.		
30.		
31.		
32.		
33.		

INVITATION LIST (Cont.)

(Bride's Relatives and Friends)

Name   *Address*

34.

35.

36.

37.

38.

39.

40.

41.

42.

43.

44.

45.

46.

47.

48.

49.

50.

51.

52.

53.

54.

55.

56.

57.

58.

59.

60.

61.

62.

63.

64.

65.

66.

INVITATION LIST (Cont.)

(Bride's Relatives and Friends)

Name	Address
67.	
68.	
69.	
70.	
71.	
72.	
73.	
74.	
75.	
76.	
77.	
78.	
79.	
80.	
81.	
82.	
83.	
84.	
85.	
86.	
87.	
88.	
89.	
90.	
91.	
92.	
93.	
94.	
95.	
96.	
97.	
98.	
99.	
100.	

INVITATION LIST

(Friends of Both Bride and Bridegroom)

Name   *Address*

1.
2.
3.
4.
5.
6.
7.
8.
9.
10.
11.
12.
13.
14.
15.
16.
17.
18.
19.
20.
21.
22.
23.
24.
25.
26.
27.
28.
29.
30.
31.
32.
33.

INVITATION LIST (Cont.)

(Friends of Both Bride and Bridegroom)

Name   *Address*

34.

35.

36.

37.

38.

39.

40.

41.

42.

43.

44.

45.

46.

47.

48.

49.

50.

51.

52.

53.

54.

55.

56.

57.

58.

59.

60.

61.

62.

63.

64.

65.

66.

INVITATION LIST (Cont.)

(Friends of Both Bride and Bridegroom)

Name   *Address*

67.

68.

69.

70.

71.

72.

73.

74.

75.

76.

77.

78.

79.

80.

81.

82.

83.

84.

85.

86.

87.

88.

89.

90.

91.

92.

93.

94.

95.

96.

97.

98.

99.

100.

SUGGESTED SUPPLEMENTARY READING FOR EACH SECTION

SECTION I: *Design for Christian Marriage* by Dwight Small, Revell, 1959.
(For the Bride) *Letters to Karen* by Charlie W. Shedd, Spire Books, 1965.
(For the Bridegroom) *Letters to Philip* by Charlie W. Shedd, Spire Books, 1969.

SECTION II: *Communication—Key to Your Marriage* by Norman H. Wright, Regal, 1974.
Intended for Pleasure by Ed Wheat and Gaye Wheat, Revell, 1977. (Tapes also available.)
Sexual Happiness in Marriage by Herbert J. Miles, Zondervan, 1967.
The Act of Marriage by Tim and Beverly LaHaye, Zondervan, 1976.

SECTION III: *The Christian Couple* by Larry and Nordis Christenson, Bethany Fellowship, 1977.
Discovering the Intimate Marriage by R. C. Sproul, Bethany Fellowship, Inc., 1975.

SECTION IV: *Financial Planning Guide for Your Money Matters* by Malcolm MacGregor, Bethany Fellowship, Inc., 1977.
Silvia Porter's Money Book by Silvia Porter, paper, Avon, 1976; cloth, Doubleday, 1975.
Your Money Matters by Malcolm MacGregor, Bethany Fellowship, Inc., 1977.

SECTION V: *After You've Said I Do* by Dwight Small, Revell, 1968.
The Christian Family by Larry Christenson, Bethany Fellowship, Inc., 1970.
What Is a Family? by Edith Schaeffer, Revell, 1975.

SECTION VI: *Why Am I Afraid to Love?* by John Powell, Argus, 1967.
Why Am I Afraid to Tell You Who I Am? by John Powell, Argus, 1969.